HUMANITY

The Illustrated Geography of Our World

Racehorse for Young Readers

· inquiries should be addressed to Racehorse for Young Readers, 307 West 36th Street, 11th Floor, New York, NY 10018. • Racehorse for ·oung Readers books may be purchased in bulk at special discounts for sales promotion, corporate gifts, fund-raising, or educational pur- ·ses. Special editions can also be created to specifications. For details, contact the Special Sales Department, Skyhorse Publishing, 307 West ·th Street, 11th Floor, New York, NY 10018 or info@skyhorsepublishing.com. • Racehorse for Young Readers™ is a pending trademark of ·yhorse Publishing, Inc.®, a Delaware corporation. • Visit our website at www.skyhorsepublishing.com. • 10 9 8 7 6 5 4 3 2 1 • Library of

HELLO PEOPLE!

Scientists think that there have been creatures like humans on the planet for two million years. But the first humans who were most like us are called ***Homo sapiens.*** This means "wise man" in Latin. Once they began to explore the world there was no stopping them—or us!

Homo sapiens lived in Africa about **200,000** years ago.

Homo sapiens **MIGRATED** (= moved from one part of the world to another)...

... probably **100,000** years ago

and **60,000** years ago.

Homo sapiens settled down and started farming about **12,000** years ago.

MORE and MORE HUMANS = VILLAGES TOWNS CITIES

250 Babies born every minute.

105 People die every minute.

HUMANS AT WORK

ARCHAEOLOGISTS look at ancient objects, bones, and buildings to find out how people lived in the past. They are like history detectives.

There are more Lego people in the world than real ones!

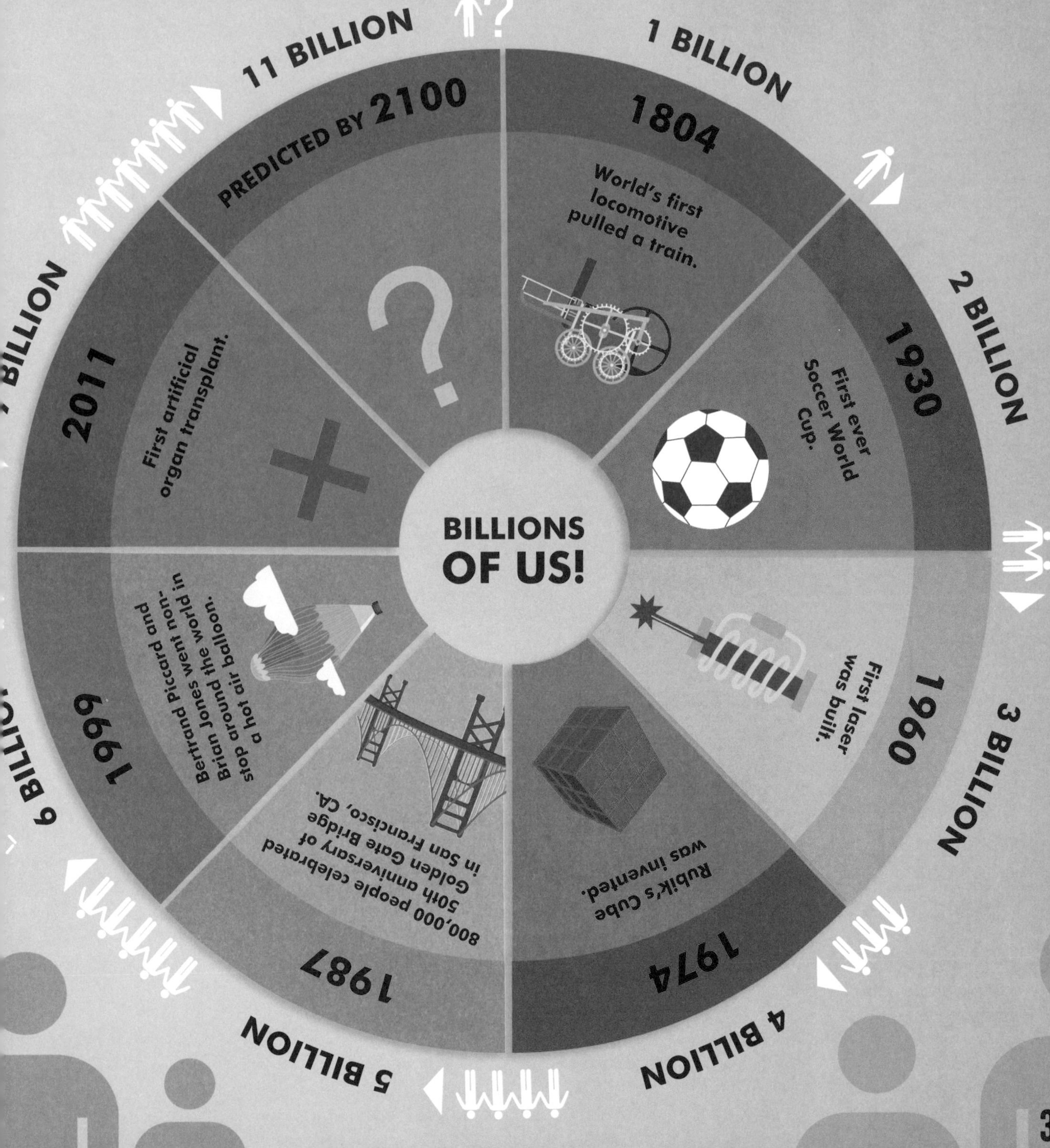

BILLIONS OF US!

1 BILLION
1804
World's first locomotive pulled a train.

2 BILLION
1930
First ever Soccer World Cup.

3 BILLION
1960
First laser was built.

4 BILLION
1974
Rubik's Cube was invented.

5 BILLION
1987
800,000 people celebrated 50th anniversary of Golden Gate Bridge in San Francisco, CA.

6 BILLION
1999
Bertrand Piccard and Brian Jones went non-stop around the world in a hot air balloon.

7 BILLION
2011
First artificial organ transplant.

11 BILLION
PREDICTED BY 2100
?

We are so lucky to have such a beautiful planet to live on. Humans make homes in all sorts of places on Earth, but if you look at the planet at night from space you can see where most of us live by looking at the lit-up areas.

7 out of 10 of the world's biggest cities are on the coast = **more than ½** of the world's population lives by the sea!

Pacific Ocean

Atlantic Ocean

THE MOST POPULATED CITIES

Tokyo, Japan = **38 million**

Delhi, India = **26 million**

Shanghai, China = **24 million**

Cities with more than **10 million** people

are called **MEGACITIES.**

MEGA = very big!

HUMANS AT WORK

DEMOGRAPHISTS (deh-mog-rah-fists) are scientists who study populations. This means they look at how many people there are, where people live, and how this changes over time.

GREENLAND is the **BIGGEST** island in the world but **LEAST** populated country **(56,000 people).**

JAPAN is DENSELY populated = 32 square feet **PER PERSON.**

Arctic Ocean

9 out of 10 humans live in the Nor... ...here.

Indian Ocean

No one lives in the middle of the **SAHARA DESERT!**

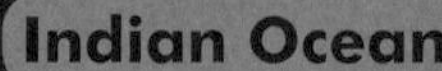

Southern Ocean

ANTARCTICA
Loads of penguins (and a few visiting scientists).

WATER TO DRINK

Humans need water and not just any old water. We need safe, clean water to stay healthy. Have you ever thought about where your water comes from and how much of it you use each day?

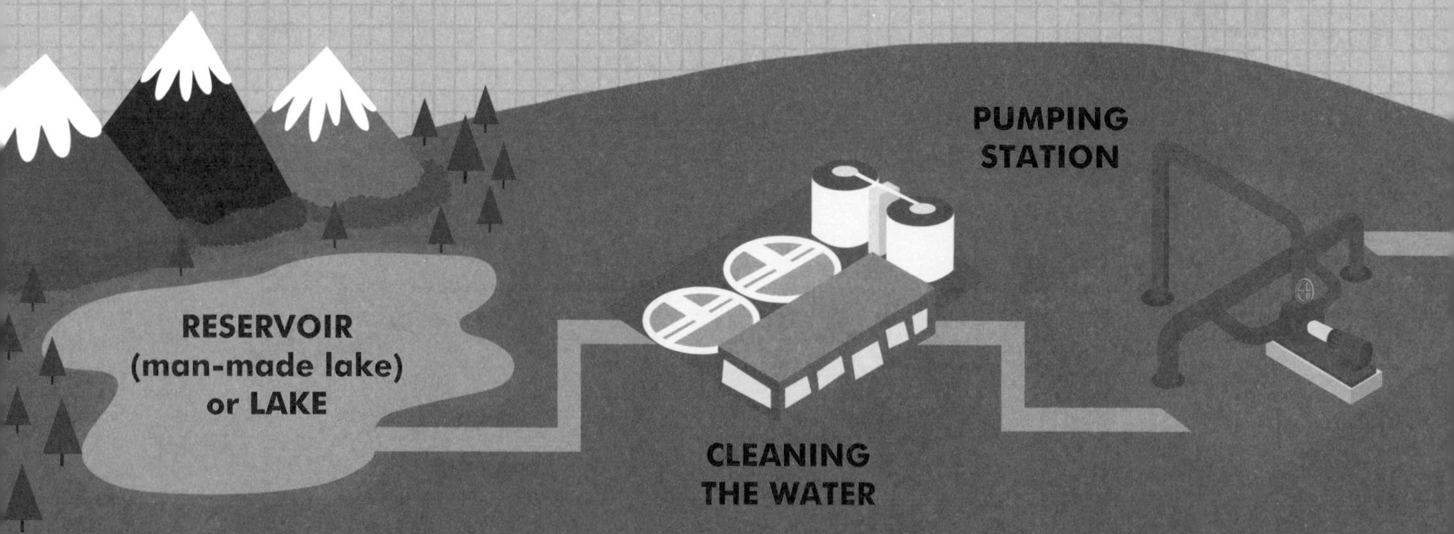

RESERVOIR (man-made lake) or LAKE

CLEANING THE WATER

PUMPING STATION

Grown-up = **60% water**

Newborn baby = **75% water**

Recommended daily water intake = **6-8** glasses

Humans cannot last MORE THAN 7 DAYS without water.

1 in 3 people on Earth **DO NOT** have safe water.

1 in 9 people on Earth **DO NOT** have a bathroom.

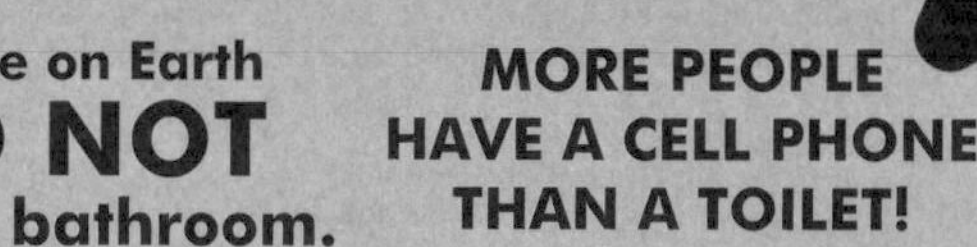

MORE PEOPLE HAVE A CELL PHONE THAN A TOILET!

HUMANS AT WORK

WATER CONSERVATIONISTS work to protect water supplies in the environment. They help to make sure that water is used carefully. It is too precious to waste!

18 gallons per shower

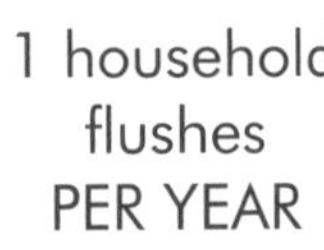

1 household flushes PER YEAR

=

350 BATHFULS

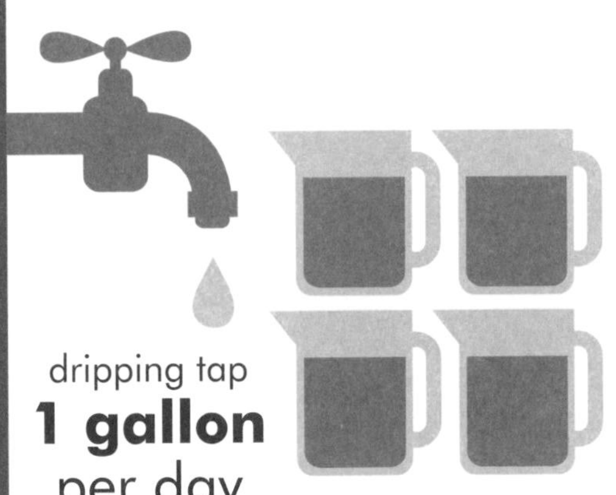

dripping tap **1 gallon** per day

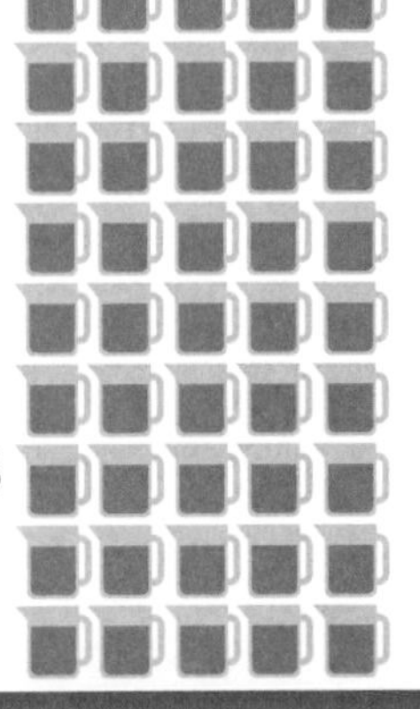

15 gallons per wash

…S TO SAVE WATER

Fix drips.

Take shorter showers!

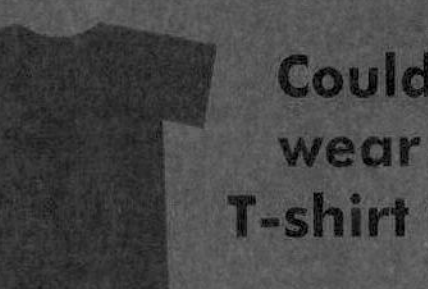

Could you wear that T-shirt twice?

THE EARTH SHOP

The world is like a giant store with countries buying and selling different things. These things are calle "resources." Some resources, like oil and gas, just happen to be in a country already. Other resources like crops or animals for food, are grown or farmed.

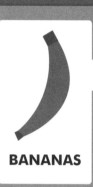

BANANAS

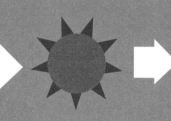

Grown in **hot and tropical** countries.

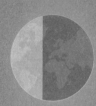

ECUADOR sells (EXPORTS) ONE THIRD of all the bananas traded in the world.

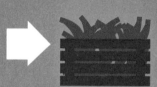

Picked and packed.

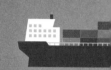

Shipped t the US in **REEFER** **(REFRIGERATED S** **in 6-12 DA**

TREES

Grown in **cold and northern** parts of the world:

Canada Finland Sweden Russia

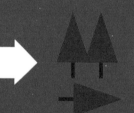

Cut down.

Loaded on to trailers.

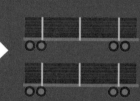

Transport

OIL

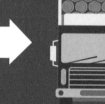

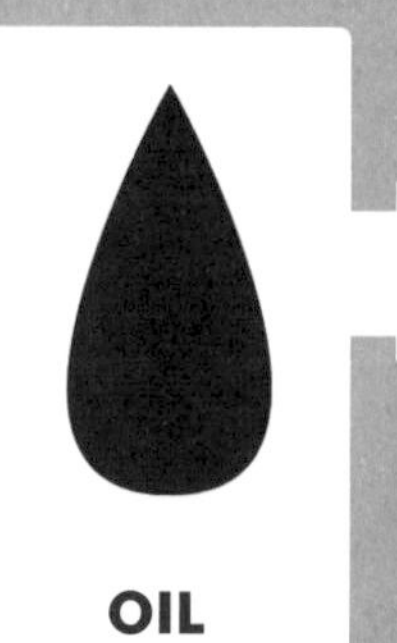

Found in the **Middle East** and **Africa**:

Saudi Arabia
Iraq
Kuwait
Nigeria

OIL WELL

PIPELINES

TRANSPORTED across the world in tankers.

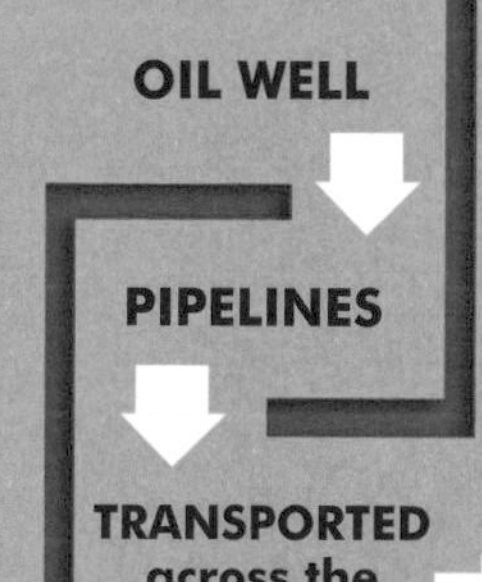

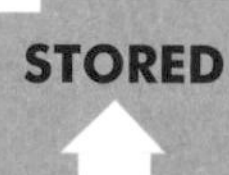

REFINED = made into gas, diesel, and oil.

STORED

Taken by road tankers and pipelines...

to **GAS STATIONS.**

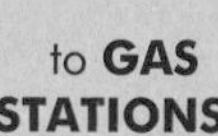

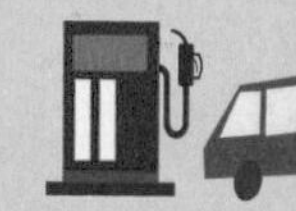

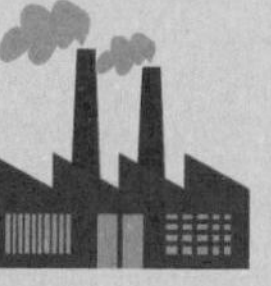

to **FACTORI** Made into pai shampoo, make and plastic.

HUMANS AT WORK

An **ECONOMIST** studies the way resources are traded or shared between people and countries. They can help people understand how to make the most of their resources and earn more money.

ETHICAL TRADING
Means that the people working on farms or in factories must be paid enough for their work. It also means that where they work must be safe for them, too.

IMPORT (buying) is the opposite of **EXPORT** (selling)

Ripened in warehouses **for 4-6 days.**

Trucked to shops.

Bought by consumers.

Eaten!

to timber mills. Made into planks for building.

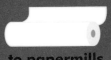

to papermills. Made into paper.

TIMBER
=
wood that is made ready to be used for building or carpentry.

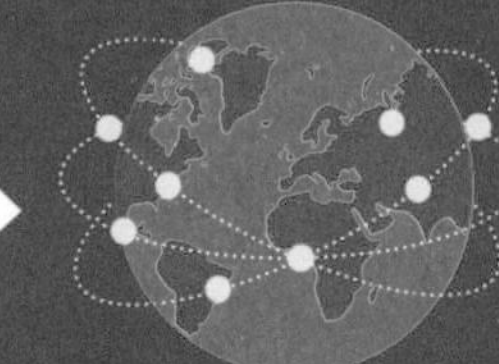

Exported all over the world.

4 billion trees are cut down each year to make paper.

60%
(two thirds)
of all oil taken around the world travels by **TANKER.**

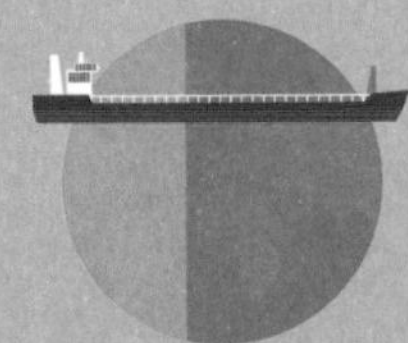

30%
(one third)
of trading across oceans is **OIL and GAS.**

LARGEST TANKER
=
4 million BARRELS of oil
=
140 million gallons

Oil is measured in **BARRELS.**

GETTING AROUND

Humans have invented many different ways to travel. We can fly far across the planet in a plane or take to the seas in a ship. We can whiz around on bicycles, motorcycles or in cars. Imagine how lon it might take to go right around the world using different forms of transport.

ROAD RAIL

WATER AIR

EQUATOR
=
24,900 miles

mph = miles per hour

HUMANS AT WORK

ENGINEERS use science to solve problems, like how to invent the fastest train. **ASTRONAUTS** are trained to travel into space to do research and explore the Universe.

Earth to Mars = 34 million miles

No human has been there yet!

6 mph TAKES 167 days

60 mph TAKES 17 days

23 mph TAKES 45 days

A ship's speed is measured in **KNOTS.**

1 KNOT = 1.15 mph

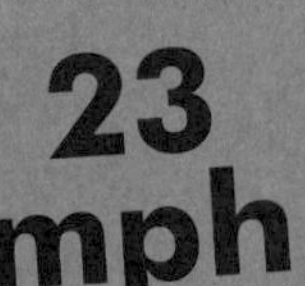

60 mph TAKES 17 days

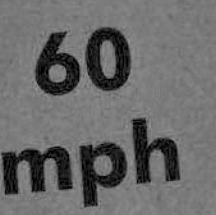

550 mph TAKES under 2 days

FASTEST TRAIN ON WHEELS

French TGV150

Top Speed = 355 mph

AMPHIBIOUS VEHICLES

These can go on land and sea.

TREASURE FROM UNDERGROUND

There are many valuable rocks and minerals under the surface of our planet. Some countries have more of certain kinds of minerals than others. This means they can trade them with other countries.

IRON

is made into steel.

cars

paper clips

beams in skyscrapers

China • Australia • Brazil • USA

ORES are rocks that contain metal. We can get that metal out by **HEATING** the rocks.

This is
called
SMELTING.

TIN

is very light and often mixed with other metals.

China = BIGGEST PRODUCER

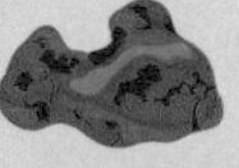

COPPER + TIN = BRONZE

METAL ORES

COPPER

is easy to bend and stretch.

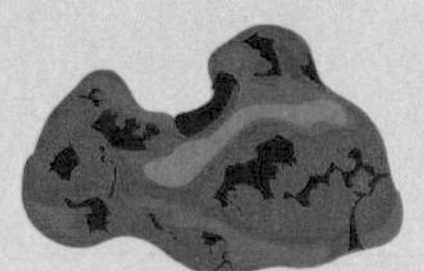

The average car contains **0.9 miles** of copper wire.

Chile has 6 out of the 10 LARGEST copper mines in the world.

PLATINUM

is the **RAREST** and most **EXPENSIVE** metal in the world. It doesn't rust or tarnish.

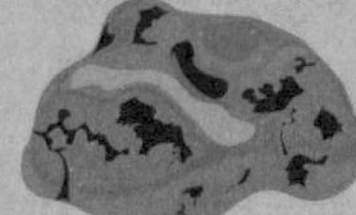

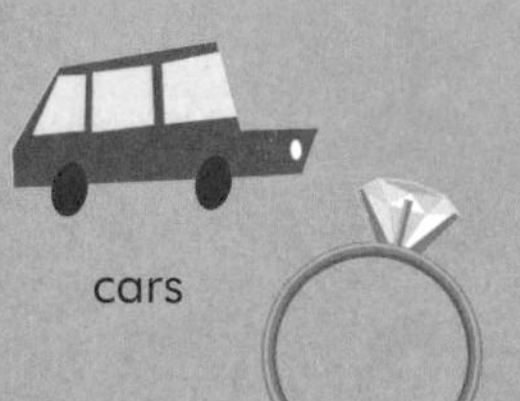

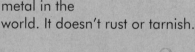

cars

jewelery

medical instruments

South Africa • Russia

HUMANS AT WORK

METALLURGISTS are scientists who study metals. They can use their knowledge to put different metals together to make strong mixtures called **ALLOYS**. This helps humans make stronger cars and airplanes.

DIAMONDS

are beautiful and extremely hard.

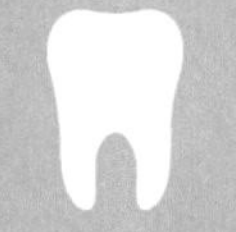

jewelery · dentists' drills · drills for oil rigs

Botswana • Russia • Canada

GEMSTONES

RUBIES

Big rubies are rarer than big diamonds.

Burma

SAPPHIRES

Kashmir
Burma
Sri Lanka

EMERALDS

Colombia
Brazil
Zambia

LVER

; bacteria so it is d in bandages.

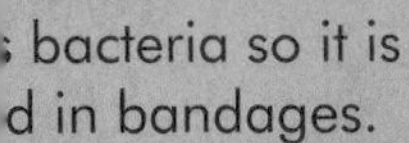

velery

silver threads in gloves to use with touch-screens

coins

Mexico • Poland • Bolivia

PRECIOUS METALS

GOLD

is shiny, beautiful, and super-useful!

It is even used for coating the outside of an astronaut's visor.

China • Australia • USA

DEEPEST GOLD MINE in the world

SOUTH AFRICA

Mponeng Mine is nearly **2.5 miles deep.**

RUBBISH!

Dumping trash and waste on land or in rivers and seas pollutes our world. This then harms people, animals, and plants. We only have one planet and we all need to look after it carefully.

We **THROW IT** in the **GARBAGE** and **FORGET** about it **BUT...**

PILES OF TRASH

There are millions of tons of trash in landfill.

Some never rots.

Some rots and gives off nasty gases.

This damages the atmosphere.

Plastic in landfill takes **500 YEARS** to rot away (decompose).

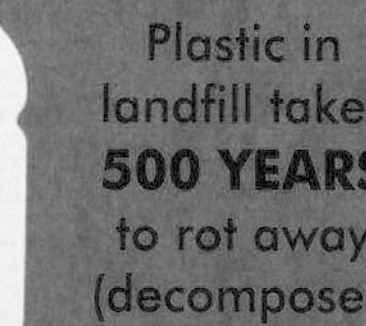

PLASTIC IN THE SEA

Plastic dumped in the sea poisons or traps fish and sea animals.

BIGGEST PLASTIC ISLAND

=

Pacific Garbage Patch in Pacific Ocean.

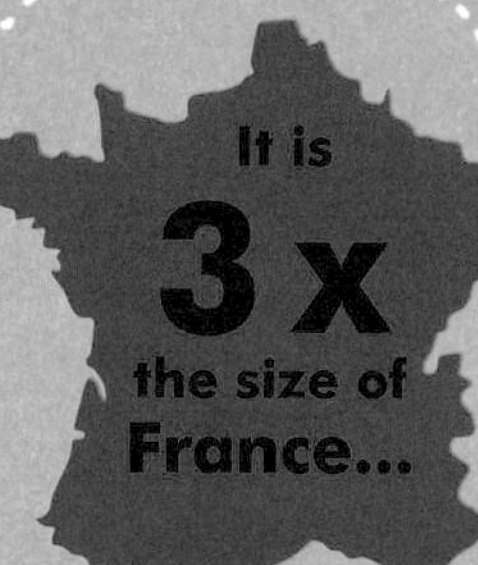

It is 3 x the size of France...

... and weighs same as

500 JUMBO JETS

This is the same as

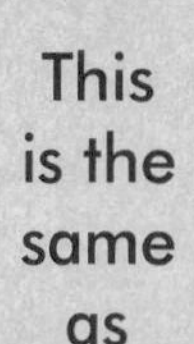

250 PIECES of trash

for **EVERY PERSON** in the world.

HUMANS AT WORK

PRODUCT DESIGNERS design all the things we use in our lives, from chairs to computers and toothbrushes to book bags! Many designers try to make sure that their designs use recycled materials.

TAKE ACTION!

Use your own bags.

Look for unpackaged items.

Buy refills.

Find out which charities recycle old cell phones or computers.

Don't buy too much stuff, like food, in the first place!

THINK BEFORE YOU THROW IT OUT! Can it be recycled or reused?

RECYCLING

25 x 2-liter plastic bottles makes 1 fleece.

1 ton of **RECYCLED PAPER** saves **17 TREES.**

FOOD CANS ARE **100% RECYCLABLE.**

GLASS IS **100% RECYCLABLE.**

Making **1 NEW CAN** uses the same energy as it takes to **RECYCLE 20 CANS.**

COMPOSTING

peelings

old fruit

teabags

uncooked veggies

garden cuttings

turns kitchen and garden waste into food for plants.

BURNING TRASH

creates energy to power lights and heating... but also harmful gases.

TOP INVENTIONS

Humans are really clever and have invented so many wonderful things. It is impossible to choose the best ones, but here is a very small selection. All of them have made a big difference to our lives.

TELEPHONE

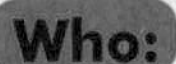

When:

1876

Who:

Alexander Graham Bell

Life-changer:

Humans can now talk to people who are not in the same room.

Fun fact:

The first cell phones were made in the 1970s.

WATERPROOF CLOTHING

When:

1823

Who:

Charles Macintosh

Life-changer:

Humans can keep warm and dry, whatever the weather.

Fun fact:

In the UK, raincoats are still sometimes called Mackintoshes or Macs.

GAS CAR

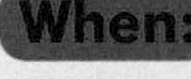

When:

1885

Who:

Karl Benz

Life-changer:

Humans can now really go places! But...

Fun fact:

Benz's first car only had three wheels!

HUMANS AT WORK

An **INVENTOR** is someone who comes up with an idea for a new gadget or a way of doing things. They can get a special licence to stop other people stealing their ideas! This is called a **PATENT**.

AIRPLANE

When:

1903

Who:

Orville and Wilbur Wright

Life-changer:

Humans can now fly!

Fun fact:

Their first flight = **120 feet** in **12 SECONDS**.

POP-UP TOASTER

When:

1921

Who:

Charles Strite

SLICED BREAD

When:

1928

Who:

Otto Rohwedder

Life-changer:

Human breakfasts are never the same again!

Fun fact:

By 1933 **8** out of **10** loaves in the USA were **SLICED.**

VACUUM-CLEANER

When:

1901

Who:

Hubert Cecil Booth

Life-changer:

Humans can clean their homes quickly and easily.

Fun fact:

The first vacuum cleaner was called **PUFFING BILLY.** It was so **BIG** it had to be pulled from house to house!

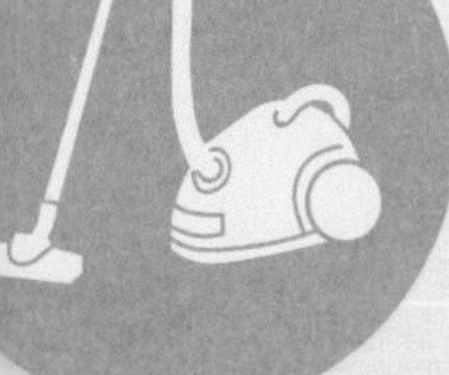

POWER ON THE PLANET

Humans use lots of electricity to power things like lights and machines.
Electricity can be made in many different ways and some of these are better for the planet than others.

ENERGY SOURCES = WAYS TO GET ELECTRICITY

Solar power

is power from the Sun.

Water power

is hydro-electricity.
NO HARMFUL GASES
but dams change the environment near them.

Wind power

turns turbines

to make electricity.

Tidal energy

The tide changes
2 x each day.
Movement of water turns generators

to make electricity.

HARMFUL GAS
=
carbon dioxid
(CO_2)

greenhous
gas

traps Sun's heat

climate chan

Renewable energy → from things that **WILL NOT** run out →

Sun

Wind

Tides

Water

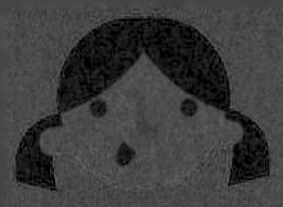

HUMANS AT WORK

ENEWABLE ENERGY SCIENTISTS work on ways to make electricity from wind, water, and sunlight. They have to think about how a wind farm will fect the environment or where is the best place to put solar power "farms."

1 ton uranium makes same amount of energy as **3.4 million gallons oil** **OR** **16,000 tons coal**

Nuclear energy

s made from a small amount of uranium.

Makes loads of electricity **BUT** also dangerous radioactive waste. **MUST** be stored safely.

Fossil fuels

These make harmful gases when burned.

Fracking

releases **FOSSIL FUELS** like gas and oil from shale rock.

It uses **LOADS** of water and may cause **SMALL EARTHQUAKES.**

HARMFUL GASES escape when fuel is burned.

Biomass energy

is electricity made by burning wood, plants, trash.

HARMFUL GASES

Non-renewable energy → from things that **WILL** run out →

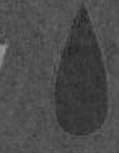

Coal **Oil** **Gas** **Nuclear**

CONNECTING THE WORLD

Today it is possible for us to get in touch with almost anyone, anywhere on the planet, immediately. We can also get loads of information at the click of a button. The internet can connect us to the whole wide world!

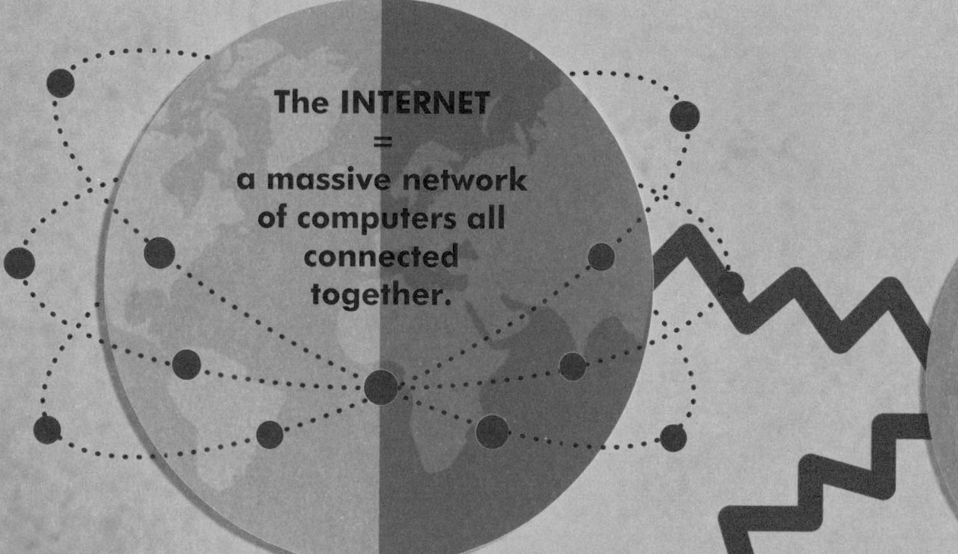

The **INTERNET**
=
a massive network
of computers all
connected
together.

The **WORLD WIDE WEB** (www or web) = loads of **WEBPAGES** you can look at using the internet.

Your computer's **WEB BROWSER** uses the **INTERNET** to find **WEBPAGES.**

A website is like a book.

Webpages are like chapters inside the book.

The World Wide Web was invented by Sir Tim Berners-Lee in **1989.**

Thanks Tim! :)

HTML =

= the language used for making webpages.

HUMANS AT WORK

COMPUTER PROGRAMMERS tell computers what we want them to do for us. They write code in languages that computers understand. Without programmers there would be no computer games!

STAY SAFE ONLINE!

Keep all your personal information private.

People you don't know are strangers. They might not be who they say they are.

If you're worried or scared tell a grown-up you trust.

VIDEO CALLING

Talk to family and friends on the other side of the world.

EMAIL

Write to your granny.

BLOGGING

Write a story or poem to share with friends. **BUT ONLY** with people you know and trust.

INSTANT MESSAGING

end messages
o your friends.

HOMEWORK!

Search the web for handy information. **BUT** check website addresses to make sure they are safe and reliable.

TALKING TO PEOPLE

Humans are very chatty animals, and it is fascinating to think about all the different languages there ar in the world. Some languages are spoken more than others. Perhaps you speak some of them yourself

SPANISH
442 million

HINDI
260 million

JAPANESE
128 million

ENGLISH
378 million

People who speak these as their **FIRST LANGUAGE.**

RUSSIAN
154 million

BENGALI
243 million

HUMANS AT WORK

INTERPRETERS translate the words that someone is saying into a different language. They help people who do not speak the same language as each other to be able to communicate. They often know lots of languages.

There are more than 7,000 languages in the world.

CHINESE
1,299 million

Which language is spoken in the most countries?

ENGLISH
(165 countries)

ARABIC
315 million

Which countries have the most **LIVING** languages?

Nigeria	**526**
Indonesia	**710**
Papua New Guinea	**841**

PORTUGUESE
223 million

ENDANGERED LANGUAGES

151 languages in the world — less than **10 PEOPLE** still speak them.

NO children are learning them — they will soon be **EXTINCT.**

HUMAN WORDS TO KNOW

ALLOY
A metal made by mixing two or more metals together. Copper and tin make bronze.

ARTIFICIAL
means something made by humans. An artificial organ is a copy of the real thing.

ATMOSPHERE
is the air all around Planet Earth.

BILLION
is a thousand million or 1,000,000,000.

CONSUMER
A person who buys things.

DECOMPOSE
means to rot away. Dead things and trash decompose.

ENVIRONMENT
is the air, water, or land that people and animals live in and on.

EQUATOR
is the imaginary line that runs around the "waist" of our planet.

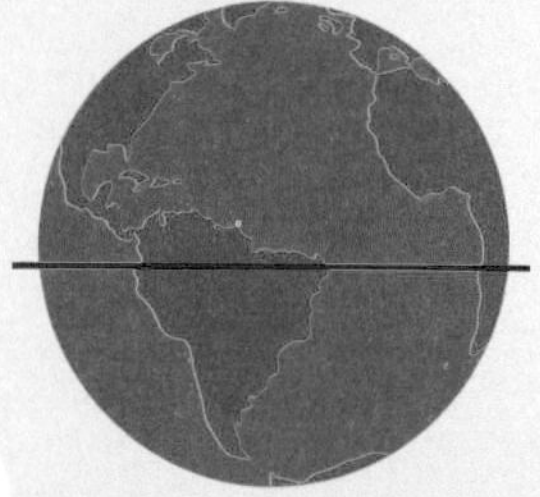

ETHICAL
means doing the right thing. An ethical consumer tries to buy things that do not harm the environment or other people.

EXPORT
means to sell to another country or part of the world.

EXTINCT
means completely dead. If a language is extinct it means that no one speaks or writes it any more.

FOSSIL FUELS
are oil, coal, and gas. They are natural fuels formed millions of years ago from dead animals and plants.

GENERATE
means to produce or make. Energy sources are used to generate electricity.

HOMO SAPIENS
This is the name given to our own modern human species.

IMPORT
means to buy from another country or part of the world.

LANDFILL
is another word for a trash dump.

MEGACITY
A megacity has more than 10 million people living in it.

MIGRATE
means to travel out of your own area to another place.

MINERAL
A valuable or useful substance that has formed naturally under the ground.

NON-RENEWABLE
means that once something is all used up there is no more of it.

ORE
A kind of rock that has useful metal inside it.

POLLUTION
When poisonous or harmful stuff is put into the environment.

POPULATION
is the number of people in a town, country, or the world.

PRODUCER
A producer makes or grows things to sell. Producers can be people, companies, or whole countries.

RECYCLE
means to reuse something by making it into something else instead of throwing it away.

RENEWABLE
means something that does not run out.

RESOURCE
Something useful that can be used by people or sold for money or exchanged for othe resources.

SMELTING
is the way that ores are heate to get the valuable metals out of them.

SOURCE
Where something comes from The source of nuclear energy is uranium.

TARNISH
is when a shiny metal loses its shine and looks dull and stained.

TRADE
is another word for buying and selling.

TRANSLATE
means to change words into another language.